JUNIOR

GRIFFEY ON GRIFFEY

JUNIOR

GRIFFEY ON GRIFFEY

Written by Ken Griffey, Jr.

Edited by Mark Vancil

Photography by Walter Iooss, Jr.

CollinsPublishers

A Division of HarperCollinsPublishers

Special Thanks to:
Michael McMillan, Anne McMillan and Paul Sheridan

At Nike Sports Management:
Lynn Merritt and Coleen Powell

At the Seattle Mariners:
Dave Aust

Produced by:
Rare Air, Ltd.
A Mark Vancil Company
130 Washington Street
West Dundee, IL 60118

Designed by:
John Vieceli
McMillan Associates

FIRST EDITION
CATALOGING-IN-PUBLICATION DATA ON FILE AT THE LIBRARY OF CONGRESS

ISBN 0-00-225219-8
97 98 99 00 01 / 10 9 8 7 6 5 4 3 2 1

For my uncle, Jim Bell, who passed away during the making of this book,
and my great-grandmother, Alberta Littleton Stanton

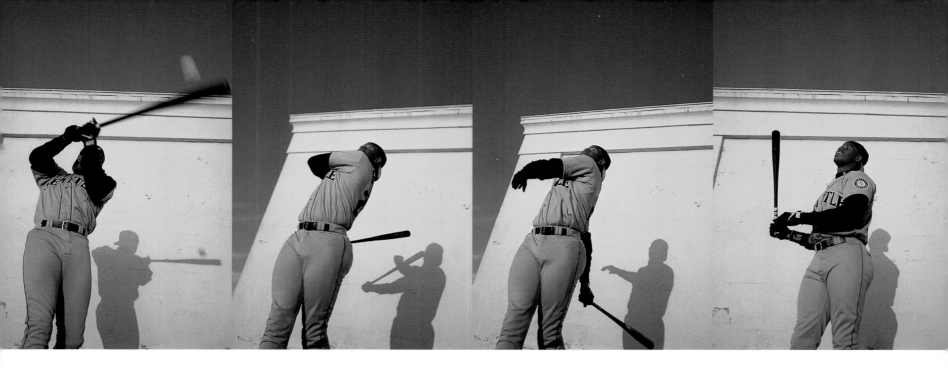

[SPRING COMES EARLY] [MY TIME] [GOING HOME AGAIN]

 10   48   90

¹⁰

Once January rolls around, my focus is completely different.

*U*ntil then, I really don't spend much time thinking about baseball. I don't spend hours hitting in a cage or lifting weights. I play golf, spend time with my family and relax. But when January comes, I'm a totally different person. I'm more moody and I have a hard time just hanging around the house. It's like my biological clock tells me I'm supposed to be somewhere else. I'll leave home about a week before I'm supposed to be at spring training just to get there and get ready.

I was 17 and a high school senior when the Seattle Mariners drafted me in 1987. It was tough leaving home for Bellingham, Washington, to start my professional career while all my friends were back enjoying their last summer before college. Not only was I a long way away, but there were a lot of expectations, being the No. 1 pick in the entire draft. When I arrived, everything was so new to me that a couple times I got into trouble with management. Sometimes it was because they didn't know me and other times I just didn't know any better. For example, I'm allergic to fish, so if I eat the wrong kind I can die. But no one knew that the night we played in Spokane. The bus ride home took about seven hours, so we had a postgame meal before we headed back to Bellingham. Since the meal happened to be fish, I didn't eat. By the time we got into town, it was four in the morning and I hadn't eaten. So I stopped at Denny's before I went to bed. Meanwhile, the coaches had a curfew check and I wasn't there. When I got to the ballpark the next day the manager called me over and started yelling. I didn't want to hear it. I told him I'd pay the fine and thought that would be the end of it. The manager didn't exactly see it that way. He called my dad and then my dad called me and started yelling. Once I explained, he understood. But I remember him saying, "They're going to tell me everything you do." And he was right. Anytime I did something wrong, I knew I could expect a phone call from my dad.

I like being in the clubhouse and hanging out
with my teammates. We'll fool around with one
another and play practical jokes, but

you never mess
with somebody's equipment.

That's sacred.

*Y*ou have to ask to touch somebody's stuff.
I don't like people using my bats.

Batting gloves?

I've got my name on those, so no one messes with them.

Fielding gloves or shoes?

No one touches my glove or my shoes.
I lock up everything, even in my own clubhouse.

I just don't like people touching my stuff.

It may sound like a superstition and there could be something to that,
but I had so many things stolen early in my career that
I don't take any chances.
Instead of throwing my jersey into the laundry with everyone else,
I give it to our equipment man personally.

My dad, Ken Griffey, Sr., and I have the identical swing. Everybody says, "Yeah, but he didn't hit home runs like you do." That's true, but he was in a different offense. He was the guy that had to move a man over, get on base and steal. He had to use his legs. With me, it's the opposite. I hit third and I'm expected to hit the ball out of the park and drive in runs. But I'm not the player he was. I'm not as good a player as my dad. People always look at the numbers, but the numbers really don't mean as much to ballplayers as they do to people outside the game. I wish I could run like my dad. I wish I could throw as well as my dad. He played right field and had one of the strongest arms I've ever seen. At one point he was the fastest man in baseball. Even when I went up and robbed Jesse Barfield of a home run in Yankee Stadium, everyone compared my catch to one my dad made. They still tease me that he got up higher than I did. He probably did. His was a better catch. So all the credit I'm given for being better than my dad, it's not true.

He was a better player.

Most people think they have to use the off-season to get stronger by lifting weights or running ten miles a day. I know what I have to do and that's stay flexible. It doesn't matter how strong you are. If you can only move 7 inches either way, then you're not going to hit the ball out of the ballpark. Now if you can move 35 inches, then you're going to have the proper leverage and quickness to knock the ball out of the park. I'm probably one of the most flexible guys on our team. I'm not that strong. I probably only bench-press about 200 pounds, but I focus on keeping myself as flexible as possible.

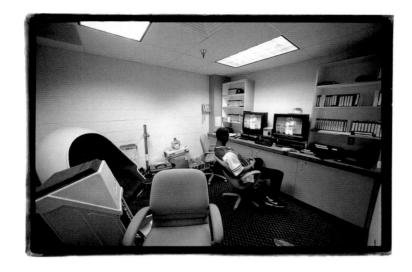

I work on my swing every day. My bat is the first thing I touch when I go into the clubhouse. That's my baby. I don't swing it much in the off-season, but I pick up a bat once in a while and just hold it. And I only watch film of my swing twice a year. I want to see how I'm swinging at the start of spring training and then again when I'm going really good. There was a big deal made of my swing in 1996 because I started out slow. The Mariners spent $5,000 on high-tech video equipment to analyze my swing and figure out what I was doing differently. It turned out to be nothing more than a minor adjustment of my hands. The computer stick-figured me and compared my swing at the time to swings I made when I was hitting the ball well. Everything was a perfect match until I started to turn on the ball. I knew something wasn't right, but all the computer can tell you is that something is different. The computer can't tell you what's wrong. I had to figure that out myself.

Most of my off-season work involves visualization. I'll think about my swing and visualize each part. I could be walking down the street or sitting in a chair at home and I'm thinking about the mechanics of my swing. I'll see where my hands are, how my weight shifts as I turn toward

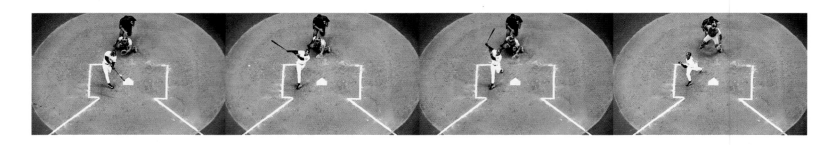

the ball. Some guys spend all winter hitting in a cage. Not me. I know my swing and I know what I have to do. Nothing changes with me. I don't have a lot of movement in the box. Instead of striding, I start out in my stride. So my at-bats always look pretty much the same.

The first few weeks of spring training are different from any other time during the year. My wife and children haven't arrived in Arizona yet, so I'm pretty much on my own. That means doing all the things most other people do, like going grocery shopping, cooking my own dinner, washing my own clothes.

My father has always been real patient with everything. He fishes, hunts, golfs; anything that requires patience he does and he does it well. Me? I'm learning to be patient because I have a son and a daughter. But it's the same with baseball. He always tells me, "Pitchers make more mistakes later in the count than they do earlier. So just be patient." He just drums that into my head: Just be patient and everything will take care of itself. He's always been that way. When he would talk to us he didn't just fly off the handle. Even if he was mad he'd ask what happened instead of yelling and screaming about the situation. Then he would let us know how he felt.

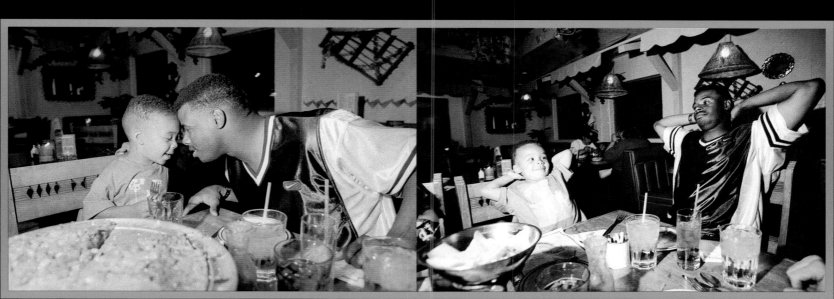

In the back of my mind, I know there are crazy people out there and that at any given moment anything can happen. I've never really been afraid at the ballpark, but when someone runs onto the field, I'm very aware of what could happen. You just never know. For the same reason, I would prefer to have my wife and children as far in the background as possible. I don't necessarily want them seen a whole lot. People know what time I leave for the ballpark every day and they know what time I get home. All they have to do is look at the schedule to know when I'm out of town.

*E*ven though my father was gone a lot during the baseball

season, he was always there for us when we were growing up.

That's something I'll never forget and something I want my

children to know about me.

He was there.

If we needed something he didn't care if we woke him up

at two in the morning. We could call him at the ballpark if we

had a problem and he would talk to us. He always told us,

"If you ever need some help, you call me no matter what

I'm doing. Baseball has always been secondary

and it always will be." It's really about how much time

I can spend with my family. My dad was a great example

because he taught me that it was all right to feel that way.

I know it's all right to feel that way.

*E*veryone involved with making my shoes takes pride in the process. And the athletes, guys like Michael Jordan, Deion Sanders and myself, are involved in every step. I start by going through the Nike catalog and reviewing the different kinds of shoes and colors. I'll choose color schemes and styles for the design department. In a few months they will have come up with some

drawings to review. A few months later the first shoes arrive. At that point my job is to wear them and let everyone know where

they need to be more snug or looser. The entire process takes around 18 months. A good example of the time from concept to

product is my 1998 shoe. I've been working on that model since just after the 1996 baseball season.

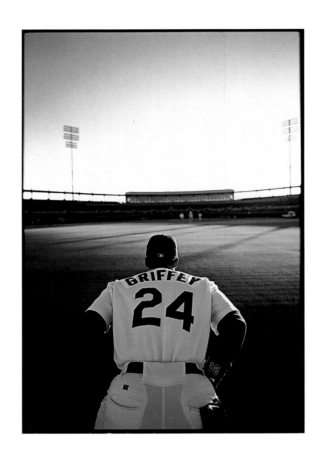

Playing center field has always been
a function of my particular abilities.
When I was 14, my high school coach looked
at what I could do and put me in center.
He needed someone that could cover some
ground out there and he knew I could run.
He also needed somebody with a good arm
and, since I had been a pitcher from
the moment I first started playing baseball,
he knew I could throw. So it made sense
to him and it's made sense to me ever since.
I genuinely like playing center field
because I feel like I can control
the entire outfield from that spot.

As I set myself
to throw, my only
thoughts are to
keep the ball down.
I want to make sure
to hit the cutoff man.
I want to make sure
I throw it far enough
out in front of him so
that if I do bounce the
ball, it will come up
about thigh or chest high.
Early in my career, base runners
challenged me a lot more. Teams
didn't know me very well, so they
wanted to see what kind of arm I had.
That doesn't happen very often these days.

Every once in a while, though, somebody will test me.

I did notice a little more
of that after I came back
from the broken wrist in
1995. But I threw a
couple guys out
and that stopped
pretty quickly.

Growing up, we didn't necessarily know when something was written in the newspaper about my father. The only way we found out was when my mother and father would talk about it around the house, because we didn't get the New York news-papers in Cincinnati. It's pretty much the same for me. Even now I don't see anything until I get to the ballpark unless I happen to grab a newspaper at my hotel. Other than that, I don't pick up a newspaper to check out what may or may not have been written about me. Everyone is entitled to their opinion, but that doesn't mean I have to read about it.

𝒯he downside to being a well-known person is the lack of time to just be myself. I get down just like everyone else. But outwardly, particularly in public, I can't be down. I understand most people look at my situation and think I have everything, so I should be happy every minute of every day. And I am, for the most part. But I'm pretty sure if I gave you my life for one month you would end up saying, "I don't know about this. Maybe this isn't what I want." I'm sure it looks easy. I get up, go play baseball, then come home and rest. But it's really a 24-hours-a-day, seven-days-a-week job. No matter what I might have done at the ballpark that night or what I might have accomplished that season, I still have to be concerned with what I'm going to do the next day or the next season. What do I have to work on? What do I have to do to come into the season in shape? What do I have to do tomorrow to get myself ready to play? And I know I'm watched all the time. I have to be aware of my actions whether I'm on the field or off. I might do nine positive things and one negative, but I know that one negative thing is going to be what people talk about. So, to some extent, you can't be yourself. I can't be loud. I can't joke around as much as I might with my family or friends because someone could take it wrong.

Signing autographs can be difficult sometimes. At any given moment, particularly around the ballpark, you could be headed to do something important for your performance. Maybe you can't stop and spend time signing at that moment. Then other times, when you are able to stop, there are just too many people to accommodate. What makes it difficult for me is that no matter how many I sign, there is always going to be somebody that doesn't get an autograph. And that one person is going to be upset.

There was an instance early in my career that really bothered me because I was blamed for something I had no control over. I had agreed to do a poster for a company in Seattle and, as far as I knew, that was the end of the deal. But they waited until my mom and dad left town before they asked if I would sign a few of the posters at a local establishment. The next thing I knew, there were radio ads about Ken Griffey, Jr., signing posters. Nobody cared about the fact that I had to get to the ballpark that day. I had been under the impression that I'd sign a few posters and be on my way. But I showed up and there were hundreds and hundreds of people and they all wanted to get a poster signed. Suddenly I was being booed and called names. I was trying to do the company a favor, then I found myself being perceived as a bad guy. One kid came up with a blue Sharpie and wrote down the side of my white Mercedes. I was 19 years old at the time and that's when I kind of went into a shell. Even now you don't see me quoted in the newspaper a whole lot. I just don't want to go through anything like that again. I don't want to be misinterpreted to that extent ever again.

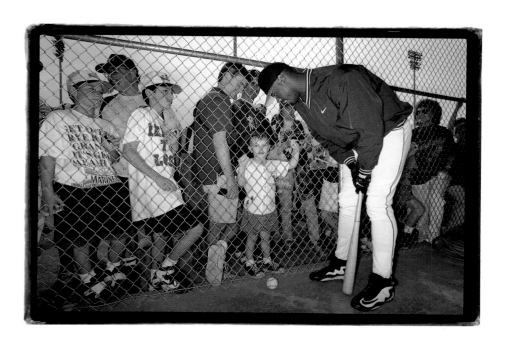

[MY TIME]

The pressure that comes from everyone's expectations of me is really something I've had all my life.

When I was in Little League, my mom had to go home and get my birth certificate to prove I wasn't too old to play. I wasn't that big, but I was kind of tall and thin for my age. We got ready to play a game one night and one of the coaches on the other team got mad and said his team would refuse to play until they saw my birth certificate. We just lived around the corner, so my mom went home, grabbed it and the game went on. In a way, playing in the Major Leagues isn't much different.

$\mathcal{I}$ always get to the ballpark early. If we've got a 7:30 p.m. game, then we'll have batting practice at 4:50 p.m.

I'll leave my house, which is only about 15 miles from the Kingdome, around two o'clock. There are usually a few

other guys that get there early, too. I'll take my time getting dressed and just relax. We'll get in a card game or

two. In just about every clubhouse in Major League Baseball you can find guys playing cards. Same thing on the

plane. It's relaxing, everybody knows at least one card game, and you don't need a whole lot of room to play.

My approach to the game of baseball isn't very complicated. I go out there every day whether I'm sick, suffering

through bumps and bruises, or tired. Even when I've been hurt, I've come back earlier than when doctors expected.

I don't want to be on the bench collecting a paycheck. I'm paid to perform and to help my team. If I don't feel

like I'm contributing, then I don't feel like I'm earning whatever I'm being paid. If the manager wants to give me a day off, that's his decision. But if it were up to me, I'd be out there every day. My job is to play. When I walk across the white lines, that's all I'm thinking about.

*I*t's my job to know as much as I can about everybody on the team and then, when I can, to help them out. The 1996 season was a good example. Alex Rodriguez and I had some strange conversations at some strange times. I remember being in the on-deck circle talking with Alex about his contract situation during a pitching change. I could look at him and tell he was worried about it. But generally I try to make everyone laugh. Obviously they can tease me. I'm not immune to that. At the start of last season, Sterling Hitchcock, one of our pitchers, called me an $8 million "Judy" hitter because I wasn't swinging the bat very well early in the year. I reminded him that it wasn't how you start but how you finish. Then, about three-fourths of the way through the season, I started

feeling a little more comfortable and I had T-shirts made that said, "Griffey in '96" on the front. On the back I had, "American League Championship Series Victims." I had the names of David Cone and John Wettland in blue and Hitchcock's name in bright red. Those were the pitchers I hit home runs off of in the 1995 playoffs. Hitchcock was one of them before he was traded from the Yankees to the Mariners. I had to get 20 of them made because everybody wanted one. It was fun and everybody gets a kick out of those kinds of stunts. It's a long season and you can get tired of looking at one another. So you have to have some fun.

$\mathcal{E}$verybody wants to know what makes me play the way I do. They say, "You don't go into the gym. You don't lift weights. You don't have this strict diet." I just know my swing. I've used the same sized bat since high school, 34 length, 31 ounces. I would experiment with my dad's bats, which were 33 x 33. But I haven't changed a lot. I think the only thing I've changed since I started playing professionally are my batting gloves. Not surprisingly, I wear Nikes now. My swing is the same. There are a few people, and they're all family members, that can look at me on the field and know if I'm doing something wrong at the plate. My mom, my dad and my brother, Craig. Once during the 1996 season we were playing the White Sox in Chicago in an ESPN game. My dad was watching the game in Colorado where he was a coach for the Rockies. Next thing I knew I had a call in the dugout from my father. He said, "They're pitching you away. Hit the ball to left field." The next time up, I hit a home run over the left-field wall off Alex Fernandez. If my dad's in the stands and I take a bad swing, all I do is turn around and look at him. He won't do anything except maybe move his head to let me know I'm pulling out. He might be 30 rows up and all I have to do is find him. I know what I did wrong, but it just helps having that confirmation.

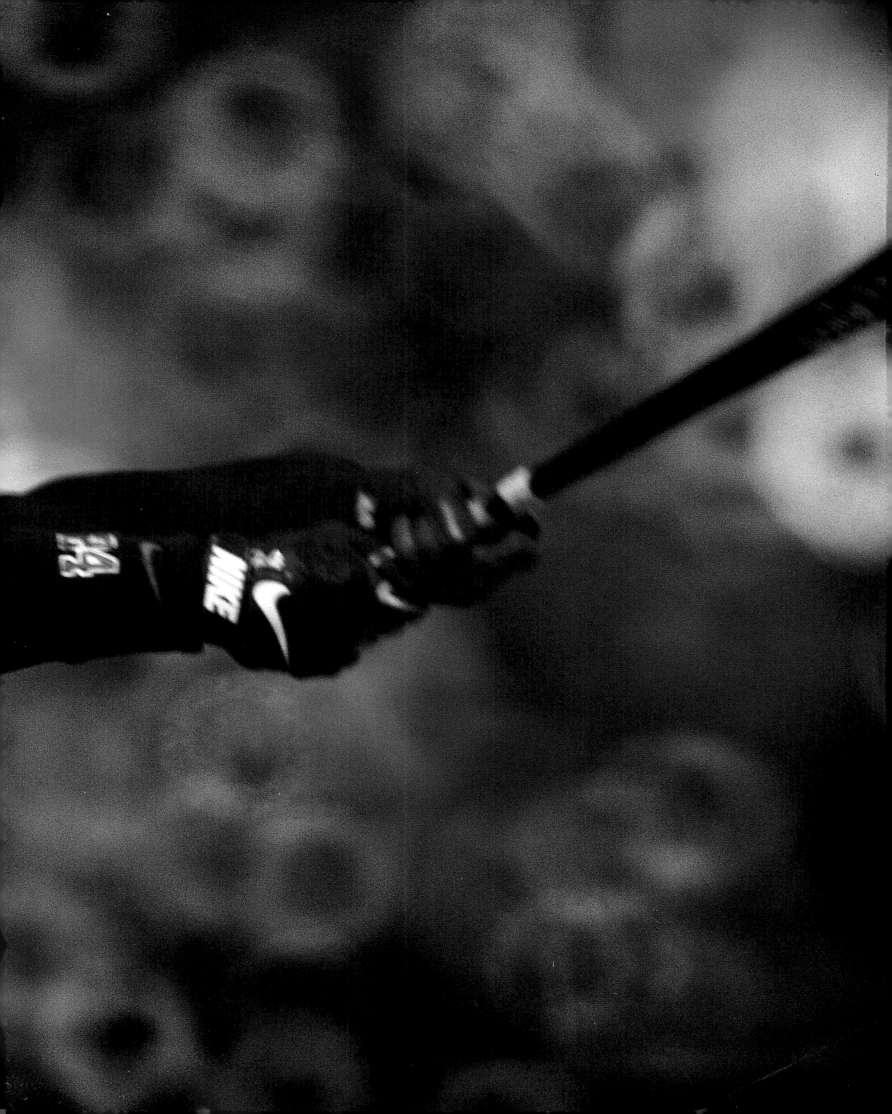

When I was a kid, I used to mimic the swings of all the Cincinnati Reds players, guys like

Joe Morgan, Cesar Geronimo, Johnny Bench, Pete Rose, Bobby Tolan.

All my dad's teammates. I was pretty good at it, too. When I was about nine, I put on my baseball uniform

and performed in a talent show. I did all the swings and afterward everyone sang, "Take Me Out to the Ball

Game." But my dad found out and he wasn't very happy. He said, "You're not them. You are my son and I

want you to swing the way you want to swing. I don't want you to be Pete Rose, Johnny Bench or anyone else."

See, my dad was a professional baseball player, so there was a little difference between me trying to be

someone else and another kid doing the same thing. He told me imitation is a form of flattery and that

I shouldn't try to be anyone other than myself. And that's true. I tell kids that now.

Don't be me.
Just be yourself.

I'm competitive at everything. I don't like to lose, whether I'm playing golf,

a video game, basketball, cards or Ping-Pong. I won't embarrass you,

but I'll try to beat you every time. I can beat you and not embarrass you. Now, if you want to start trash-talking, then I think I'm pretty good at giving it right back.

A few years back, former New York Yankees manager Buck Showalter talked about how disrespectful I was by wearing my hat backward. The truth is I didn't start wearing my cap backward to be stylish. I started wearing baseball caps that way because I wore my father's caps when I was growing up. The bill bounced down over my eyes and I couldn't see when I ran, so I turned it backward. From the age of about 5 until I was 14, I still couldn't fit into my father's caps, so I always wore them backward. Showalter was one of those guys that thought I just turned my cap around after I got to the big leagues. He said I wasn't wearing the uniform correctly and, according to him, disrespecting the game. But it just happens I grew up wearing my hat backward. I don't tell anyone else how to wear their uniform. In fact, I don't say anything to anyone about anything. If I don't like someone, I don't say anything. That's just my way. I don't jump on people if they make a mistake, because I don't want them doing that to me. As far as Showalter is concerned, he doesn't know me. He doesn't know what I'm about or why I wore my hat backward. Times have changed, the game has changed. Look at those old news reels of Babe Ruth. He'd hit a

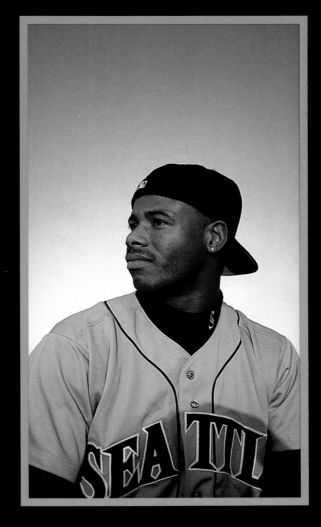

home run and tip his hat to the fans as he ran around the bases. Do that now and you'll get hit by a pitch the next time up. On the other hand, you can look at the ball for a second as you walk halfway down the first base line and nothing happens. Even the uniforms are different. Uniform pants used to be up high and baggy. Now they're long and tight. And everybody's got different shoe companies and sponsors. It used to be that everybody looked the same. Now they don't. There's nothing negative about that. It's just the way things are today. Wearing a hat backward or having a gold chain around your neck has nothing to do with how much or how little anyone respects the game.

The dugout is like the clubhouse.
It's a place I feel comfortable.
If I don't want to do anything,
then I don't have to do anything.
There are no outside demands or distractions,
just you and your teammates,
the manager and the coaches.

The pressure was a little tougher on me than it's been on my teammate Alex Rodriguez. The positive for Alex is that he can go out and play. The negative is that he doesn't get the kind of recognition early in his career that he deserves. He will, but it will take longer. It's like Michael Jordan and Scottie Pippen. It took a lot longer for Pippen

because Jordan was around. In much the same way, my situation was different than that of Alex. From Day One, they labeled me the "Savior of Baseball" in Seattle. With Alex, you heard about how he was a great shortstop that could come in and help Ken Griffey. But I've talked to Alex and told him not to worry about what's being written. Never believe all the good things and then wonder why they're writing the bad things.

I always tell people I got to know my teammate Jay Buhner really well because of all those meetings in right center field during pitching changes. Really, we're so different that you wouldn't think we'd get along as well as we do. I like rap music, he likes country. He wears Wrangler jeans, I wear Guess.

I have hair, he doesn't.

There are just certain things about Jay that make him who he is, and I like those things. For example, I mentioned to him once that I liked a certain Garth Brooks song. He went out and bought me the CD. You get to talking and find out about people. Everybody looks at Jay and thinks he's intimidating. But when it comes to his family, he's a big baby. He's got another side to him that fans don't really see. And when it comes to family, I'm just like Jay.

My
approach to

hitting is pretty simple.

I figure
the pitcher's
got 18
inches
of plate
to work
with.

If he's
going to
get me out,
then he's going
to have to
throw at
least one pitch
over the plate.
See the ball,
hit the ball.

Baseball is a game in which everyone focuses on numbers, from batting average to runs batted in to hits and home runs. For fans, the game revolves around these numbers. But as a player, I really don't concern myself with the statistics. I'm thinking about what I can do to help my team win. That's it. But my numbers have to be different from everyone else's. Who would think I could miss 20 games in 1996 and still hit 49 home runs and drive in 140 runs? Who would think I could hit 26 home runs and drive in 80 runs after breaking my hand? If I'm hitting third and doing my job to help the team win, then my numbers have to be bigger. Look at Michael Jordan. You see him make a few shots during the

course of the game and all of a sudden it's halftime and he's got 30. So when I hit 40 home runs or drive in 120 runs, people expect that. I know my numbers have to be totally different to merit special attention. But any time you hit .285 or better, hit 20 or more home runs, or drive in 80 or more runs, you've helped your team. It doesn't mean you have to hit .350 or drive in 150 runs. Would you rather have a guy that hits .250 or a guy that hits .350? Everybody would say the .350 hitter. But what if the .250 hitter has an on-base percentage of .450? And what if the .350 hitter has an on-base percentage of .375? Now who do you want? See, the numbers really don't matter. What matters is what you do to help your team win. Numbers are for everybody else to look at.

If I had to pay to watch one player, then Kirby Puckett would be the one I'd go to see.

Kirby is by far my favorite player.

He's got a 5-foot-8 frame, weighs 220 pounds and he could hit anybody anywhere. In center field he could go get any ball and he'd jump over that wall in Minnesota and bring one back if he had to. And you never heard his name involved in anything negative. The first time I saw Kirby in the big leagues, I was just 19. But he walked over and said, "Welcome to the big leagues. Keep a smile on your face, have fun and play hard. You're going to be here awhile." Kirby could hurt you with one swing of the bat, but it was still fun to watch him go out into the field because you didn't know what he was going to do. You never saw him frowning. Kirby was always smiling at the ballpark. Even after the death of his mother, which was hard on him, Kirby found a way to be positive. I told him our whole family was sorry for his loss and gave him a big hug when we were in Minnesota. He said, "You know, she's still with me wherever I go. This way she can see me every day. She can see me play and run around. Before, she couldn't see me play every day. Now she can and that's important." That's just the kind of guy he is.

Would I play again?

*W*hen I broke my wrist in 1995, the first thing I asked the doctor was whether I'd be able to play again. I wanted to know right then and there. Would I play again? My hands and wrists are 90 percent of my game and I knew the injury was serious the minute I pulled away from the wall. Kevin Bass hit a ball toward the right-center-field wall in Seattle. I'd made a catch once before where I'd stopped myself by putting both feet up the wall as I made the play. This time my hand turned the wrong way as I braced myself and my left wrist shattered. My wrist looked like a spring because one part was going up and the other side was going down. Imagine your arm extended straight out and suddenly it's bent the wrong way. That's what it looked like. I rubbed it a little at first, but hit a nerve and nearly jumped out of my skin. As it turned out, the wrist was broken in 15 places. There were bone chips and fragments around the nerve and in the joint. Doctors told me a one-inch bone had been compressed to about one-fourth of an inch. Then, in 1996, the hammet bone in my right hand snapped as I checked a swing. After what I'd been through the year before, I knew there was something wrong. And it turned out to be wrong all season. Although I had a career-high 49 home runs and drove in 140 runs, the hammet bone injury affected me all season. Doctors had to move the nerves to remove the bone. The result was a loss of feeling in my pinky and sometimes through my whole right hand. I'm sure some days people just figured I had a bad day. That might have been the case, but more often it was because I just couldn't feel the bat. My hands are a big part of my life, so on any given day I was anywhere from 65 to 90 percent healthy.

I know some people look at the way I play the outfield and think I'm crazy running into walls or diving all over the place.

But that's just the way I was taught to play. If something happens, then I'll worry about it later. I can't change. I'd quit the game before I'd change my approach. If I had to think about diving for a ball or chasing one into the outfield wall, then I wouldn't be the player I am today. If I can get to a ball, then that's what I'm going to do. I don't believe in half-stepping or pausing. Every athlete will tell you that's inviting injury. The guys going full speed all the time aren't the ones getting hurt. It's the guys trying to avoid injury that are most likely to be injured because that approach isn't natural. My first game back from the broken wrist in 1995, I crashed into the wall making a catch. I never even considered the possibility of having any fear. I understand the downside. If I were to break my wrist that way again, it could be a career-threatening injury. But I'll worry

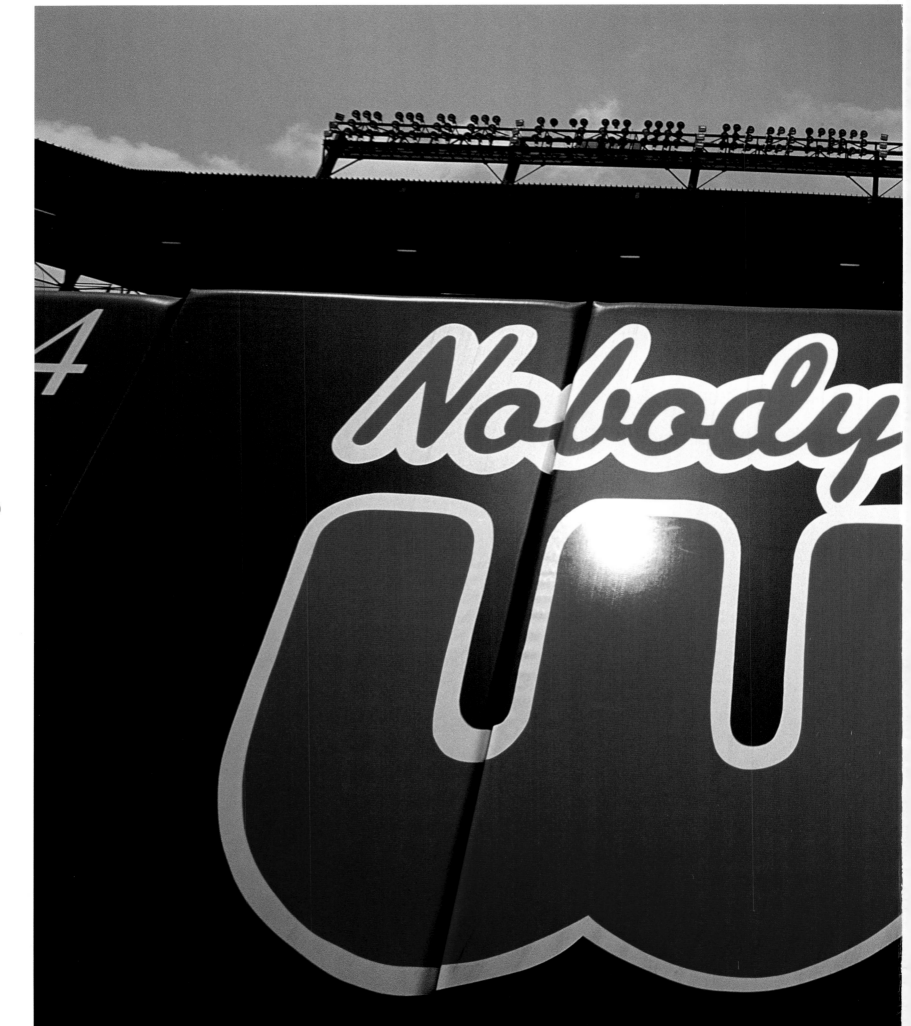

I was the first son of a Major Leaguer to be the No. 1 pick in the amateur draft. Then, in 1990, my father and I became the first father-son combination to play together in the same outfield. That experience, playing alongside

my dad in the Major Leagues, is something I'll never forget. I went out and got gold bracelets made for each of us. I

had "First Father and Son" inscribed with rubies, diamonds and sapphires. It looks like a championship boxing belt.

The only thing I would do different than my dad is to move the family with me if I was traded. We stayed in Cincinnati those years my dad played in New York and Atlanta. I can understand where my dad was coming from with regard to New York. He said, "No, you're not moving there." But I think if it were anywhere else, we should have gone. Then again, it was kind of fun when my dad was away because every time he'd come home he had something for us.

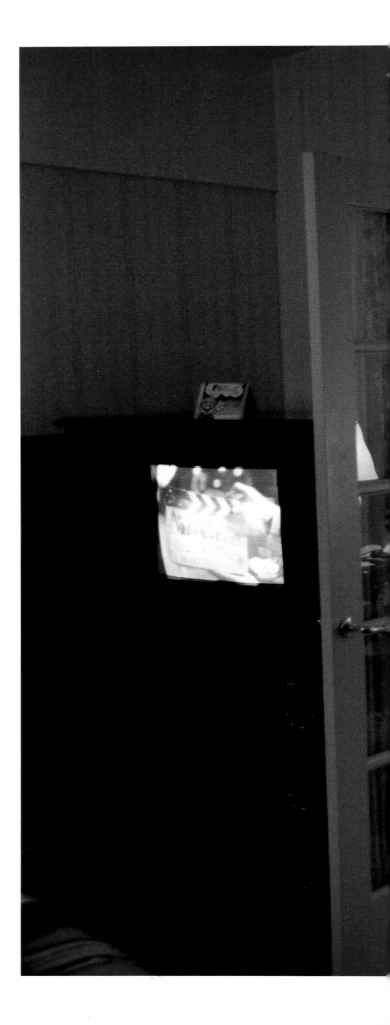

I know that no matter what happens, to them I'm just Ken.

Having that kind of strong family relationship does help me on the baseball field. I know that no matter what happens, good or bad, I still have them. To them I'm just Ken or Daddy. They want me to succeed just as I do. But my success or failure at work doesn't change how we all feel about one another. So many people worry about being famous or playing out the role that they lose sight of what's happening at home.

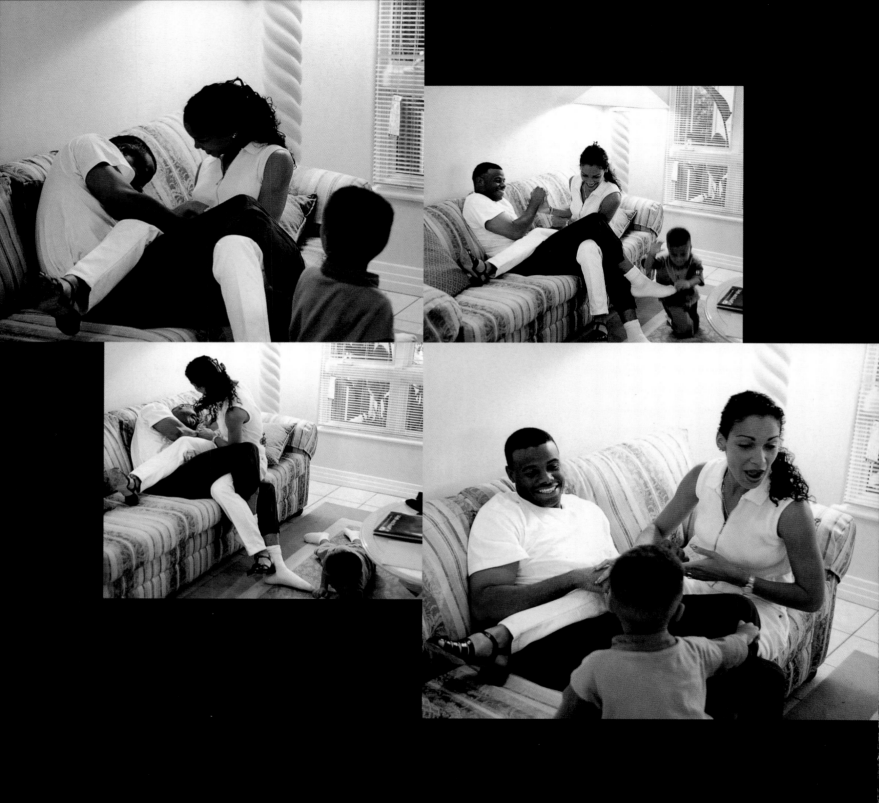

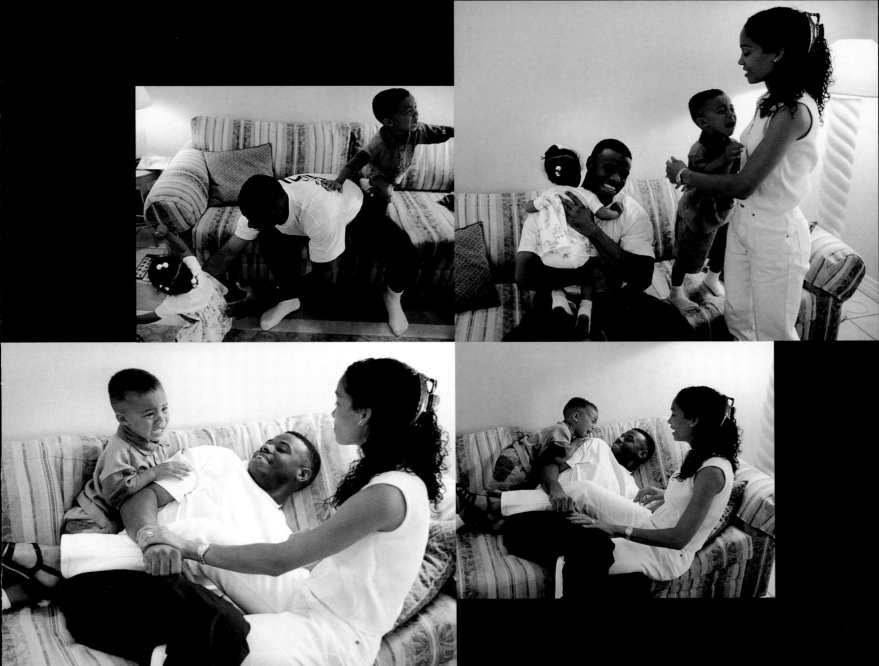

Having a daughter has probably been more of an adjustment for me than for my wife, Melissa. I grew up with a younger brother so my parents could buy one toy and we'd both play with it. But even at these ages—Trey is three and Taryn had her first birthday in January—they are totally different. I feel like I have a football player and a cheerleader. She's definitely taught me to be a softy. When Trey gets upset or frustrated and starts crying, I have a tendency to let him work through the problem. With Taryn, I'll pick her up right away. With my son, I guess I think about myself as a kid. I figure he's a little tougher because he's a boy and a little older. But with my daughter, it's a lot harder to see her cry. And I think she's already figured that out.

I got married when I was 22. I met my wife, Melissa, when we were both 19. She's an athlete, so she has the same kind of stubborn mentality I have. She played soccer in high school, she'll ride jet skis, ride four-wheelers, shoot basketball, roller-blade, bowl, play tennis and golf. Everything I like to do she likes to do, except fish. I haven't taken her fishing yet. That seems like more of a man thing. Melissa and I met at an under-21 club in Seattle where she asked me to dance. I said, "Wait a minute," and she said, "No, you have to get out there and dance." We ended up talking all night and then she politely called me at 7:30 the next morning, which was only about four hours after we each got home. I talked to her for about 20 minutes before I realized who it was because I was so tired. I'm not real good at talking on the phone early in the morning. But after that first night, we were together three years, and then we were married. It was the perfect thing to do. It wasn't like, "Oh no, I'm getting married." It wasn't like that at all. We're more like best friends. She can go anywhere and do anything she wants. About the only time my wife gets mad at me is when I won't go somewhere. If there are going to be a lot of people, like at a mall or a grocery store, then I'd rather stay home. It's not that I don't like talking with fans or meeting new people, but when I'm with my family, I'd prefer to give my attention and focus to them and not be bothered. I'm very fortunate because I have a great family. I'm just glad Melissa asked me to dance.

have any problem relaxing, especially in the off-

My parents always told me there were only a few players that ever make it as professional athletes. They told me

to make sure I always had a backup plan just in case baseball didn't work out. And my plan was to go to college

study mechanical drawing and become an architect. The new house we're building in Orlando is something

helped design. Most houses are flat, just straight up and down. I always wanted a house that was shaped almost

like a V so people couldn't look into my backyard. I designed two wings at almost 45-degree angles. My interest

in design and architecture started in seventh grade when we had to make a house out of Styrofoam and cardboard

I play as much golf as I can, even during the season when my schedule allows. I only recently started playing the game seriously. Before 1994, I played in a few tournaments, but I was really just stepping up to the ball and swinging to see how far it would go. Everything I hit was long.
Then the whole family—Melissa, my dad, my mom, Craig, his girlfriend and I—took lessons in 1989. I play at about a 12 handicap, but I think I'll get better the more I play.

The thing I like about golf is the fact that

I'm out there
by myself.

Even though I might actually be out

there with three other guys,

I'm really just playing against myself.

My parents always tried to make things fun.

Even on the day my dad got out of his cast following knee surgery, we went right out tossing. I was a pitcher, so my dad stood at the plate and I threw pitches to my brother, Craig, who was the catcher. I was afraid to throw inside because I might hit him in the knee. But my dad stood right up on the plate. I swear if he would have uncurled his big toe it would have been right on the plate. He was that close. So I wouldn't throw the ball inside. He kept telling me, "Close." So I threw one a little too inside and hit him right on the knee. I don't know whether he went down to the ground, but I do know I cried. After that I wasn't afraid of throwing inside. I ended up hitting four batters in a row in the next game I played, but I wasn't afraid anymore.